amazing but true golf facts

amazing but true golf facts

Bruce Nash and Allan Zullo

Compiled by Larry Dorman

P. COKER, JR.

Andrews and McMeel

A Universal Press Syndicate Company

Kansas City

Library of Congress Cataloging-in-Publication Data
Nash, Bruce M.
    Amazing but true golf facts / Bruce Nash and Allan Zullo ;
  compiled by Larry Dorman.
      p. cm.
    ISBN 0-8362-7994-8 : $6.95
    1. Golf—Miscellanea. I. Zullo, Allan. II. Dorman, Larry.
  III. Title.
  GV967.N36   1992
  796.352—dc20   92-4992
                                                          CIP

Designed by Rick Cusick
Illustrated by Paul Coker, Jr.

First Printing, March 1992
Fourth Printing, February 1995

Attention: Schools and Businesses

Andrews and McMeel books are available at quantity discounts with
bulk purchase for educational, business, or sales promotional use.
For information write Andrews and McMeel, 4900 Main Street,
Kansas City, Missouri 64112.

dedication

To my friend, Julian Compton, with joyous
memories of those amazing golf "matches"
we played on our incredibly makeshift
Florida State University "course."
—Bruce Nash

To David Spicer, who belongs on the
leader board of friends.
—Allan Zullo

To my children, Emily, Tom, Chris, John,
and Rebecca, who are as amazing as
anything in this book.
—Larry Dorman

ACKNOWLEDGMENTS

There are several people without whom the material for this book never could have been assembled.

Many thanks go to Lois Hains of *Golf Digest,* who is the absolute (and final) authority on all rare and odd records in the game of golf. Also, thanks go to the editors at *Golf Magazine* for some of the items from their Wayward Wisdom section.

Golf writers who lent capable assistance are: Bob Drum, Dawson Taylor, Dick Taylor, James Diaz, Tim Rosaforte, Bob Green, T. R. Reinman, Steve Hershey, Melanie Hauser, and Edwin Pope.

Finally, thanks to Chris Dorman for the moral support.

contents

It's incredible that a golf ball so small can produce consequences so great. The exquisite joy and extreme pain that the game dishes out have made this timeless sport so much a part of life that the Chinese are now arguing with the Scots over who really invented it.

At least there's one thing that can't be disputed—golf is an amazing sport. A 6-year-old boy and a 95-year-old woman have each scored an ace. A duffer once needed 156 putts to hole out and a pro never three-putted throughout an entire tournament season. One golfer nailed back-to-back double eagles while another linksman was hit by back-to-back drives that ricocheted off the same tee marker.

The game has given us so much to talk—and write—about. Incredible incidents. Hilarious happenings. Fantastic feats. Remarkable records.

This book is a celebration of people, places, and events in golf that we hope will astound, baffle, and amuse you. Like the 103-year-old golfer who shot his age . . . the intrepid pair who golfed all the way from San Francisco to Los Angeles . . . the Australian who walloped a drive one and a half miles . . . the blind woman who drained a hole in one two days in a row . . . the pro who became so enraged over his poor putting that he ripped apart his car.

Golfers, to paraphrase Art Linkletter, do the darnedest things. They have from the moment the first Scottish shepherd (or was it a Chinese warlord?) hit a stone with a crook.

—BRUCE NASH & ALLAN ZULLO

hole-y toledo!

The hole in one is the most thrilling shot in golf. It is the one shot every golfer wants to hit and every spectator wants to see. But the odds are pretty good you won't make or see an ace in your lifetime.

In fact, the odds of an amateur making a hole in one on any given hole are 12,600 to 1. In other words, you have a better chance of winning a typical Pick Four lottery (10,000 to 1) or of being hit by a car (11,000 to 1) than hitting the ball into the hole with your tee shot.

Nevertheless, holes in one occur all the time, sometimes in the strangest and most astounding ways.

The Four Aces

On a cool, overcast day at Oak Hill Country Club in Rochester, N.Y., on June 16, 1989, golf history was made. For the first time ever in the United States Open Golf Championship—indeed, for the first time in the recorded history of golf—four players scored a hole in one on the *same* hole during the *same* round! It was a feat so spectacular, so astonishing, that it stunned fans and players alike.

"It was the most phenomenal, eerie thing I've ever been around in golf, and I've been around golf all my life," said pro Doug Weaver, whose seven-iron shot kicked off the parade of aces. It was 8:15 a.m. when his tee shot went into the cup at the 6th hole, which measured 159 yards.

Weaver's shot began a one-hour-and-50-minute hole-in-one chain reaction unlike any in the annals of golf. At 9:25 a.m., another roar went up from the gallery, this time for Mark Wiebe's perfect seven-iron into the cup. Twenty-five minutes later, Jerry Pate hit his Titleist No. 3 with a seven-iron. Bull's-eye—into the hole. At 10:05 a.m., Nick Price watched in amazement as his seven-iron shot landed eight feet to the right of the pin, jumped forward, and then rolled back into the cup.

The odds of a PGA Tour player making a hole in one during a given round are 3,708 to 1. But four in the same hole in the same tournament? Harvard mathematics professor Joseph Harris calculated the odds at 1,890,000,000,000,000 (1.89 quadrillion) to 1. According to his figures, there's a better chance of a golf ball suddenly leaping into the air by itself by random atomic collision than of golfers scoring four aces on the same hole in the same round.

Fanciful mathematics aside, there had been just 17 previous U.S. Open holes in one since the USGA began keeping such records in 1938. Within two hours, the Fab Four had produced roughly 25 percent of that total.

> **"In Japan, a player who scores a hole in one while leading the tournament always loses. It's a proven jinx."**
>
> —PRO AYAKO OKAMOTO

"What happened today was like some incredible fabrication," Price said. "If I hadn't been here, hadn't been part of it, I wouldn't have believed it."

Said Weaver, who heard the crowd's shouts of amazement after the aces by Wiebe and Pate: "It was pretty clear that something real awesome was going on. The electricity was all over the golf course. I just wish I could have seen them all go in."

One person who saw it all was George Siefert, a marshal at the hole. "It was electric," he said. "Impossible to believe."

Could it ever happen again? Not likely. Said John P. Everhart, the president of the National Hole in One Foundation: "What happened is mind-boggling. Four holes in one on the same hole in the same round will statistically not happen again for 190 years."

So, tell this one to your grandchildren, because in all likelihood it won't happen again until *their* children have grandchildren.

A Fine Premonition

Ron Fine of Newburgh, Ind., is no fortune-teller. He doesn't read tarot cards or consult horoscopes. But he was overcome by a premonition on the evening of July 28, 1990, as he perused the thoroughbred entries for Ellis Park Race Track in Henderson, Ky. He made a prediction to his wife that he was going to score a hole in one the next day in the second round of a member-guest event at the Shelbyville (Ky.) Country Club. He was led to this rather unusual conclusion because he noticed a horse named Hole in One was scheduled to run at Ellis Park the day of the tournament.

"I should bet on that horse," he told his wife.

The next day, Fine, an eight-handicapper, aced the 179-yard 7th hole just as he had predicted. Astonished and happy, he suddenly remembered about the horse. He had forgotten to make a wager. Hole in One, of course, won. He paid $11.80 in the seventh race.

Amazing Age-Defying Aces

* *Youngest Boy*—Tommy Moore, 6, in 1968 at the 145-yard 4th hole at Woodbrier Golf Course, Martinsburg, W. Va.
* *Youngest Girl*—Brittny Andreas, 6, in 1991 at the 85-yard 2nd hole at the Jimmy Clay Golf Course, Austin, Tex.
* *Oldest Man*—Otto Bucher, 99, in 1985 at the 130-yard 12th hole at the La Manga Club, Cartagena, Spain.
* *Oldest Woman*—Mrs. Earl Ross, 95, in 1986 at the 110-yard 17th hole at The Everglades Club, Palm Beach, Fla.

Crazy Ace

There are lucky holes in one that skip through a greenside bunker and pop into the hole. And there are those perfectly hit shots that fly straight into the cup without ever touching a blade of grass. However, none will match the wacky, unbelievable ace that was hit in 1959 at the Cotswold Golf Club in England.

Amateur John Remington was playing the par-3 7th hole with a five-iron. Remington, a mid-handicapper who had never aced a hole in his life, had no reason to believe he would record a hole in one—especially when his tee shot turned into a screaming snaphook that whistled toward a drainage ditch to the left of the fairway.

But then his ball took a remarkable journey. First, it ricocheted off a drainage pipe and skittered across the grass toward the greenside bunker, where it bounced off a rake. Then the ball popped onto the green and began rolling straight toward the ball of Remington's fellow competitor. Amazingly, Remington's ball glanced off the other ball—and plopped right into the hole for an incredible ace!

Twin Aces

Back-to-back holes in one on the same hole occur about once a month across the United States, a startling statistic in itself. But the most unusual double dose of perfection occurred in 1990, when twin brothers each aced the 2nd hole at the Scott County Park Course in Gate City, Va.

Barry Wolfe and Jody Wolfe, identical twins who were 15 years old and 16-handicappers at the time, accomplished the feat. First Barry selected a six-iron and stepped up to the tee. He rifled his shot onto the green and into the hole. Then Jody, also using a six-iron, smacked his shot into the hole right on top of his brother's ball! It was the first ace for each of the Wolfe boys.

Forget the Handicap

Margaret Waldron nailed a hole in one two days in a row in 1990. What made this feat even more amazing was that Margaret was 74 years old, suffering from severe arthritis, and was legally blind!

The Jacksonville, Fla., woman—who lost her vision to an eye disease in 1980—relied on her husband Pete to describe the direction of the hole, distance, and wind conditions. On March 18, at the Long Point Golf Course on Amelia Island, Fla., Pete lined her up on the par-3, 87-yard 7th hole. He advised her to use her seven-iron. She did—and scored an ace.

"We hugged and I felt a great sense of fulfillment," recalled Margaret. "That night, Pete and I celebrated."

The next day's ace was like a rerun of the first. Pete lined her up on another short par-3, handed her a seven-iron, and told her to take a nice, easy swing. She did and nailed the hole in one.

"When we went back to the clubhouse, I was so proud," said Margaret. "I don't consider myself handicapped. I am challenged to do the best I can with what I have."

Amateur Karen DiSabella, of Stonington, Conn.,
who in 1984 aced the first hole she ever played:

"I was worried about the people behind me getting mad because I would play so slow."

It's a Miracle!

Experts say the odds of scoring a hole in one on a par-4 hole of more than 300 yards in length increase exponentially with each 10 yards over 350. Imagine the incredibly miniscule chances of scoring an ace on a 447-yard hole.

Believe it or not, that's precisely what happened in 1965 at the appropriately named Miracle Hills Golf Club in Omaha, Neb. Robert Mitera, a man of small stature (5-foot-6 and 165 pounds) but of prodigious strength and luck, blasted a drive on the 10th hole that went the distance—all the way into the cup! It is the longest recorded hole in one in history. In fact, it's 10 yards longer than the farthest drive ever hit in a sanctioned long drive competition.

Mitera's shot was aided by a tail wind of about 50 mph and a sloping, downhill fairway. But those facts do little to diminish his amazing feat.

Other Record Aces

- *Longest by a Woman*—393 yards, Marie Robie, 1st hole, Furnace Brook Golf Course, Woolaston, Mass., in 1949.
- *Most in a Career by an Amateur*—59, Norman Manley, Long Beach, Cal.
- *Most in a Career by a Pro*—49, Mancil Davis.
- *Most in one year*—11, Dr. Joseph O. Boydstone, Bakersfield, Cal., in 1962.
- *Most on one hole*—13, Joe Lucius, on the 15th hole (yardage varied from 127 to 152), Mohawk Golf Course, Tiffin, Ohio.

Two-Timer

In Rapid City, S.Dak., DeAun West was playing in a 1991 tournament at Arrowhead Country Club where a new Cadillac was being offered for a hole in one. West promptly aced the 129-yard 2nd hole only to find, much to her chagrin, that the car would only be given away for a hole in one at the 12th hole. "I thought my luck had run out," West recalled.

But no. Incredibly, at the 148-yard 12th hole, her tee shot homed right into the cup for another ace! "I have not come down to the ground yet," she said. "This is unreal."

Less than a week later, Rick Ponto, who had never aced a hole in 13 years of playing golf, scored two holes in one on the same day. The aces came during a scramble tournament at the Serenoa Golf Club.

A Losing Ace

This from the annals of the all-time downers: Dick Downey, a 13-handicapper, aced the 170-yard 6th hole at Oakmont (Pa.) Country Club with a four-iron in 1991. He quite naturally assumed he was going to win the hole from fellow competitor Les Gallagher.

Wrong! Gallagher, a 22-handicapper, sliced a five-wood that somehow managed to bounce into the cup for another hole in one. Since the 6th hole was the ninth handicap hole, Gallagher was allowed to take off a stroke. That meant his score was zero. And that also meant Downey had lost the hole—even though he had aced it!

The Ace That Wasn't

Sharon Barrett hit her drive into the hole during the 1988 MasterCard International Pro-Am, but unfortunately, the ace never showed up on her scorecard.

Barrett's first tee shot on the 18th hole hooked badly to the left. Fearing the ball was lost, she teed up again and nailed the ace. However, the first ball was found and Barrett was forced to play it. She ended up with a bogey.

Walter Hagen, after betting ten dollars
he'd make a hole in one, and then making the ace:

**"The trick is to know when that
one time is about to happen."**

dangerous lie-aisons

To most everyone, golf is a quiet, leisurely, recreational pursuit that is as safe, relaxing, and harmless as watching television in your living room. But the truth is that golf is a lot more dangerous than you think.

Breaks of the Game

One minute, English pro Richard Boxall was playing in the third round of the 1991 British Open, three shots behind the leaders. The next minute, he was on the ground screaming in pain.

Boxall collapsed in anguish after completing his swing of a drive. Spectators said they heard a loud crack, as though a large branch had snapped. What had snapped was Boxall's left leg. He was carted off the course in an ambulance and rushed to the hospital.

Boxall's freak mishap is one of the most serious golf course injuries in a major championship. There have been many others.

In the 1988 U.S. Open at Brookline, Greg Norman took a vicious cut at an iron shot only to recoil in pain after his club hit a rock. Doctors discovered he had torn a tendon in his wrist. The Shark was out for two months.

Early in 1991, Mark Calcavecchia got his golf club caught up in a branch while taking a swing at a ball and tore tendons in his wrist. Calcavecchia, who had been one of top 10 money earners on the tour for four straight years, plummeted to near 40th in the standings by year's end.

Killer Courses

The most astonishing and tragic death from a golf ball occurred in the summer of 1914, when a soldier was hit in the temple by an errant shot at Wormit Golf Course in Fifeshire, England. The soldier, Private David Barnet, was with the 4th Black Watch, which was in training and only days away from departing for France to fight in World War I. The soldiers were training in a field adjacent to the golf course where a women's competition was underway. One of the contestants pulled her tee shot, striking Barnet in the temple. He died two days later.

His was by no means the only fatal accident on the golf course. Numerous other deaths have been recorded on the links, often from deadly injuries caused by heads flying off clubs and striking playing partners. One of the freakiest fatalities occurred in 1951. Edward M. Harrison was playing alone at Inglewood Country Club in Seattle when the shaft of his driver broke. On his follow-through, the sharp end of the split shaft pierced his groin. Harrison tried to stagger back to the clubhouse, but he collapsed and bled to death 100 yards from the 9th tee where the accident happened.

In 1963, Harold Kalles of Toronto, Canada, was mortally wounded when his throat was cut by a golf club shaft that broke against a tree as he was trying to play out of a bunker.

Lee Trevino, after being struck by lightning during a tournament in 1975:

"There was a thunderous crack like cannon fire and suddenly I was lifted a foot and a half off the ground . . . Damn, I thought to myself, this is a helluva penalty for slow play."

Unfairway Mishaps

- An overzealous fan gave a congratulatory handshake to Gary Player after the final round of the 1962 Masters and squeezed so hard that Gary thought it was broken. Fortunately, it was only sprained. But the next day in a playoff, Gary, playing with a bandaged hand, lost to Arnold Palmer by three shots.
- Pro golfer Peggy Wilson was really teed off after a driving mishap forced her out of contention in a 1969 tournament in Miami. The first-round leader was struck in the eye by her own tee when it sailed backward after she hit her drive. The bizarre injury blurred

Wilson's vision and she faded to a 78 for the round—bad enough to finish out of the big money.

• While taking a practice swing on a municipal course in Ohio in 1974, Bob Russell sent up a cloud of smoke and felt a searing pain in his leg. The club head had set off a .22-caliber bullet that somehow had been buried in the turf. Luckily, Russell was only grazed.

• At the 1957 Bing Crosby National Pro-Am at Pebble Beach, pro "Champagne" Tony Lema made a teriffic chip shot on the cliff-dwelling 9th hole. He was so excited that he leaped high into the air. But Lema landed on the edge of the cliff and tumbled backward, sliding 18 feet down the side. Fortunately, all that he bruised were his shins, elbows—and ego.

Not So Sweet Swings

• Amateur Bill Thomas scored a "hole in three" on one wild drive—he nailed two pickup trucks and a car. At the Salishan Golf Course in Gleneden Beach, Ore., in 1991, Thomas sliced his drive onto Highway 101 and hit the three moving vehicles! The ball broke the windshield of a car, caromed into the windshield of a pickup, and then smacked into the canopy of another truck. No one was hurt and the damage was covered by insurance. Said Thomas: "I think I'll change my grip."

• Faye Shelbourne was using her grandmother's antique clubs during a 1988 round of golf in Victoria, British Columbia, when she discovered they don't make 'em like they used to. As she went into her backswing, the club head flew off and smashed through a window of the pro shop.

• Actor Barry Fitzgerald accidentally decapitated his Oscar while he was practicing his golf swing in his house. Shortly after winning the 1944 Best Supporting Actor award for his role of the kindly priest in *Going My Way,* Fitzgerald took a practice swing in his den and hit the coveted statuette, which, because it was wartime, was made of plaster. Paramount paid $10 to replace it.

The Club that Swung Back

There isn't a golfer alive who hasn't felt like choking his driver. Wayne Levi actually did choke his driver—and it retaliated!

Levi, who was attempting to qualify for the U.S. Open in 1977, felt optimistic. After 34 holes in the 36-hole qualifying event, he needed only to finish with two pars to make it into the field for the biggest tournament of the year.

"I told myself, 'Don't do anything stupid,'" said Levi.

Naturally, such advice rarely is heeded, especially on the golf course. On the very next hole, Levi whacked a dreadful snap hook that had a flight pattern shaped like a jumbo shrimp. The ball flew out of bounds. Bogey was a certainty; double bogey was more likely.

Levi was livid. He angrily gripped his hands around the neck of his driver and began to strangle it, shaking it in front of his face. Unfortunately, Levi shook it a little too hard. The shaft flexed and the head of the driver smacked him right in the mouth!

The impact loosened a tooth and cut his lip and blood began spurting down the front of his shirt. The embarrassed Levi missed the cut. The cut he did make needed to be closed by a doctor at the scorer's tent.

Augusta National chairman Hord Hardin, after suspending play in the 1983 Masters because of lightning:

"We don't want to get anybody killed. Of course, if we could pick which ones, it might be a different story."

Watch the Birdie!

In 1958, Sam Snead was on a goodwill tour of South America with Jimmy Demaret when The Slammer was confronted with unexpected danger.

Snead was settling in for a bunker shot at a course in Colombia when Demaret screamed at him, "Look behind you!" Bearing down on Snead was a huge ostrich with its beak open and looking to attack. At the time, Snead didn't know that the ostrich was the club pet and probably only wanted a piece of the golfer's straw hat. All Snead knew was that this was a birdie of which he wanted no part.

So Snead threw up his arm to protect himself and the ostrich clamped down hard on Sam's hand. His fingers were so sore after the bite that he couldn't play golf for two weeks. It was the only serious injury of Snead's long golfing career.

That's the Way the Ball Bounces

Bad bounces are the bane of a golfer's existence. They can be a real pain—in more ways than one.

In 1923, the secretary to the Japanese Embassy in London was playing golf at Chiselhurst, a wonderful old course designed by Willie Park, Jr. The secretary, Mr. Wakasugi, teed up his ball and whacked it with all his might. The ball slammed directly into a post and flew straight back—and smacked into the golfer's forehead. The impact knocked him unconscious.

Forty years later, Jim Armstrong of Phoenix was playing at the Desert Forest Golf Club in Carefree, Ariz., when he accomplished a most unusual daily double. Armstrong's tee shot at the 2nd hole struck a tee marker and rebounded straight back, striking him in the head and rendering him momentarily senseless. When Armstrong recovered a few minutes later, he reteed the ball and drove his next shot—only to watch it hit the same marker! This time, the ball flew back and smacked him in the knee. That was enough pain for one day. Armstrong limped off the course.

In 1936 at Victoria Golf Club in Cheltenham, Australia, Karl Klinger hit a drive that struck a telegraph pole and rebounded behind him. Under the local rules, he was permitted to drop and hit again, which he did. Unbelievably, his second shot hit the same pole and rebounded into Klinger's face—and fractured his nose!

> **"I've injured both my hands playing golf and they're okay now. But my brain has always been somewhat suspect."**
>
> —Pro BOB MURPHY

Murder Most Fowl

Shooting birdies obviously is a desirable thing to do when playing golf. Killing them, however, is another matter.

A Washington, D.C., physician lost his cool in 1979 at Congressional Country Club, and was hauled in front of the court for murdering a goose. Witnesses said the doctor, who shall remain nameless, attacked and killed the goose with his putter when it honked during his putt on the 17th green. The putt was for birdie. The doctor missed.

The doctor hired lawyer John Dean of Watergate fame to defend him. In his defense, the physician claimed that he merely was performing euthanasia on the bird after it was seriously injured by his approach shot. He was acquitted.

The doc is not the only golfer to literally hit a birdie. In 1986, Tom DeFulvio was playing at the Avalon (New Jersey) Golf Course when his second shot on the par-5 4th hole killed a pair of blackbirds that had just taken flight from the fairway in front of him.

English pro W. J. Robinson did better than a birdie—he scored a cow! On the 18th hole of a 1934 match at the Kent Golf Course, Robinson's tee shot struck a grazing cow square on the back of the head, killing the animal instantly.

That Sinking Feeling

In a 1931 tournament in Rose Bay, New South Wales, Australia, D. J. Bayly MacArthur stepped into a bunker and suddenly began to sink. The golfer, who weighed about 200 pounds, struggled to escape the clutches of the bunker but couldn't get free.

Desperately, he shouted for help as he sunk deeper and deeper. Not until he was up to his armpits did he get rescued. An investigation revealed the sand in the bunker had turned into deadly quicksand!

Double Trouble

In the first round of the 1952 Los Angeles Open, amateur Bud Hoelscher made one of the craziest pars in the history of that storied old tournament.

Hoelscher ripped his approach shot to an elevated green and it flew over the putting surface, striking a cameraman on the head. The ball ricocheted hard, careening off a can of water and slamming into the face of the greenside announcer.

The sheepish Hoelscher arrived at the green to find a blood-spattered ball sitting about 40 feet away from the hole. After seeing that his two victims only required Band-Aids, the golfer regained his composure in time to two-putt for par.

calling long distance

Ever since the first Scottish shepherd struck a stone with his crook, man has been fascinated by the idea of hitting the ball far. The farther the better. Never mind all those axioms about how distance isn't important—"Drive for show, putt for dough." We want the long ball!

Long hitters are held in awe. They are given nicknames like "Big Cat," "Long John," and "Wild Thing." Their feats are measured by yards, not scores. Scores are for championships.

Long John

At the 1991 PGA Championship in Carmel, Ind., a star was born and a monster created. John Daly, a struggling 25-year-old rookie on the PGA Tour, bludgeoned into submission Crooked Stick Golf Club, one of the longest courses ever played in a Grand Slam event. He put on a display of raw power the likes of which had never before been seen on the major championship golf scene. After starting the week as the ninth alternate, Daly won by three shots.

The rookie did it with drives that carried unbelievable distances—he averaged 304 yards off the tee. And he did it by hitting iron shots that traveled up to 30 percent farther than those of the average touring professional. On a golf course that measured 7,289 yards—a layout Jack Nicklaus described as "the hardest golf course I've ever seen"—Daly routinely outdrove his playing partners by 100 yards. He hit drives to places on the golf course that architect Pete Dye never believed anyone would reach.

On one 525-yard, par-5 hole, Daly used a driver and a six-iron. At a 469-yard, par-4 hole, he socked a 340-yard drive and a 159-yard wedge. And he reached the 180-yard 13th hole with a nine-iron. That's not just long. That's cosmic!

When Nicklaus saw a replay of Daly's swing and was asked to analyze the secret to Daly's monstrous distance, the Golden Bear replied, "Goodness gracious, what a coil, what an unleashing of power. I don't know who he reminds me of. I haven't seen anybody who hits the ball that far."

Neither had anyone else. Daly once had a measured drive of 379 yards in Hogan Tour competition in 1990. To put it in perspective, that's longer than any winning drive in the 17-year history of the National Long Drive Championship, a competition whose sole purpose is to identify the longest driver in the world.

"I've never really thought about what gives me the length," said the 5-foot-11, 175-pound Daly. "I've always swung hard at the ball. I guess it's just a gift." One that a lot of people would pay anything to possess.

Average Distances

	JOHN DALY	AVERAGE PRO	DIFFERENCE
Driver	300 yards (plus)	260 yards	40 yards
3-wood	280 yards	240 yards	40 yards
1-iron	265 yards	230 yards	35 yards
2-iron	250 yards	220 yards	30 yards
3-iron	240 yards	210 yards	30 yards
4-iron	225 yards	200 yards	25 yards
5-iron	210 yards	185 yards	25 yards
6-iron	195 yards	175 yards	20 yards
7-iron	180 yards	160 yards	20 yards
8-iron	170 yards	150 yards	20 yards
9-iron	165 yards	135 yards	30 yards
Wedge	150 yards	120 yards	30 yards
Sand wedge	130 yards	105 yards	25 yards

"What other people may find in poetry or art museums, I find in the flight of a good drive."

—ARNOLD PALMER

Daly Redux

Just to be certain that John Daly wasn't just a one-time phenom with the driver, a national magazine tested his long-hitting skills under ideal conditions. A week after his win at the 1991 PGA Championship, *Golf Digest* took him to an airport runway at Denver to see how far he could hit a ball. The plan was for Daly to hit the ball in the thin, mile-high air, and let it land on a concrete tarmac where it could bounce and roll.

Daly rocketed his longest drive straight down the runway. It landed nearly 360 yards away and then bounced and rolled another 450 yards until it came to rest 808 yards away. More amazing, though, is that in all his drives that day, he never missed the fairway, er, runway.

Really Trucking

The longest recorded drive from the back of a pickup truck was hit in 1964 in Australia. George Bell, a member of the Penrith Club in New South Wales, was competing in the annual "King of the River" contest when he used a two-wood to drive his ball all the way across the Nepean River. The carry was certified at 309 yards. No roll was measured. And, no, the pickup wasn't moving, either.

He's Lied about the Longest Drive Ever

It gets very lonely in Antarctica. Hour after hour, there's nothing but cold and snow and penguins. Why, it's enough to make a meteorologist do something crazy, like . . . like . . . trying to drive a golf ball across an ice floe!

In 1962, an Aussie named Nils Lied decided he wanted to make a name for himself in the golf world. So Lied teed it up at the weather station at Mawson Base and looked out over the smooth, frozen ice covering the bay. Then he drove the ball with a powerful swing. The ball sailed in the frigid air, landed on the ice about 225 yards away, and then rolled . . . and rolled . . . and rolled.

The ball finally stopped 2,640 yards away—a gargantuan drive of one and a half miles! No one has ever come close to matching Lied's stupendous drive.

Arnie's Tower of Power

Arnold Palmer knew how to make his presence felt in France even if he didn't know how to speak the language. As a publicity stunt in Paris before the 1977 tournament for the Lancome Trophy, Arnie whacked some very big tee shots.

He took a sleeve of balls to the second stage of the Eiffel Tower, about 300 feet high, and drove out over the Parisian streets. Palmer's first drive traveled 403 yards after it landed on the pavement and bounced down the street.

But Arnie saved his best for last. His final drive moved right to left before plummeting to the street where it took a big bounce and landed on the second deck of a moving open-air bus!

Putting the Wood to It

Pro Craig Wood, admired for his stylish swing, never was known as a long-ball hitter off the tee. But all that changed during the 1933 British Open when he belted the longest drive on European soil and certainly the longest in the 120-year history of the championship.

At the Old Course at St. Andrews in Scotland, Wood astonished everyone—including himself—by driving the ball from the tee to the bunker about 100 yards short of the 5th hole. That's a prodigious poke of 430 yards.

To be sure, the wind was howling off the Firth of Forth and the ground was harder than a bookie's heart. Nevertheless, in the more than half a century since, no one has come close to clouting a drive that far in a major tournament.

Blowin' in the Wind

In a tournament called the U.S. National Seniors Open in 1974 at Las Vegas, amateur Michael Hoke Austin hit what might be the longest drive ever struck in an official competition. With a 35 mph wind at his back, Austin slammed his drive an astounding 515 yards.

> *"I'm hitting the woods just great. But I'm having a terrible time getting out of them."*
>
> —Pro HARRY TOSCANO

> *"Anytime a golfer hits a ball
> perfectly straight with a big club,
> it is, in my view, a fluke."*
>
> —JACK NICKLAUS

Playing at 50 Percent

With everyone looking for ways to hit the ball longer, it might seem a little strange for someone to come up with a way to hit the ball shorter. But that's exactly what Jack Nicklaus and his MacGregor Golf Co. did in 1985. Known as Cayman Golf, the concept was born because of skyrocketing real estate costs and shrinking parcels of land to develop on the Caribbean island of Grand Cayman.

In short, the game was half-golf. A Cayman ball traveled exactly half the distance of a regular golf ball, meaning a 130-yard hole was now a par-4 and a 250-yard hole was all the par-5 you could ever want.

At the opening exhibition on the island's Britannia Golf Course, Nicklaus stepped up to the tee with his driver and smashed his tee shot . . . all of 140 yards down the fairway.

The crowd went wild. "This is the first time I've ever had anybody applaud a 140-yard shot with a driver," Nicklaus said. "But I really did hit it hard. What I missed were the ooooohs and the aaaaahs."

There weren't many of those when it came to Cayman Golf. The concept, not surprisingly, never caught on big.

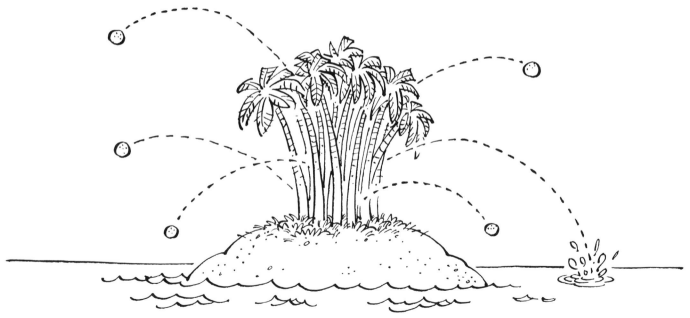

putt to the test

Putt is a four-letter word, and for golfers the world over it can turn into a vulgar scene. The putt may be the most frustrating shot in all of golf.

For sheer putting ineptitude, perhaps no one will ever approach the "feat" accomplished by amateur A. J. Lewis, at Peacehaven Golf Course in Sussex, England, in 1890. To hole out on one green, Lewis needed an astounding 156 putts!

But the greens have also been the site of some of the most astounding shots ever made.

A Fiery Stackhouse

Lefty Stackhouse, a touring pro in the 1930s, was one of the most emotional golfers who ever lived. Nothing made him more irate than missing an easy putt. He was especially provoked by putts that lipped out.

On one particularly trying day on the greens, Lefty missed five putts inside three feet and shot 81. Stackhouse was fuming so much that he wanted to vent his anger on something big that he could hit. He chose his prized possession—his Model T Ford. Stackhouse loved his Model T, which he drove to all the golf tournaments. It was the one thing that he could count on, the one thing that never let him down.

But Lefty was so enraged after his poor putting that he shattered the windshield of

his beloved car, ripped off the door, and slashed the seats. Still in a rage, Stackhouse then opened the hood and began dismantling the engine. By the time his anger had eased, the car was nearly destroyed. "I felt better after that," Stackhouse said years later. "It was unavoidable because it was the first thing I saw big enough to handle my anger for as mad as I was."

Queen of Clubs

Frances Hirsch, 69, has won more club championships than any other woman in history. Her 44 club titles are not likely to be matched any time soon. She has been club champion 25 times at Brentwood Country Club in Los Angeles, 17 times at Tamarisk Country Club in Rancho Mirage, once at the Canyon Country Club in Palm Springs, and once at the Oak Ridge Country Club in Hopkins, Minn., where she won her first title in 1951. Incredibly, Hirsch has used the same blade putter for each of her victories over the past 40 years. In a classic bit of understatement, Hirsch said, "My putter has been very good to me."

> *"The devoted golfer is an anguished soul who has learned a lot about putting just as an avalanche victim has learned a lot about snow."*
>
> —DAN JENKINS, Author

Q. What is the largest single green in the world?
A. The fifth hole at the International Golf Club in Bolton, Mass. The green has an area larger than 28,000 square feet—enough room for three typical three-bedroom houses with yards.

You're Putting Me On

There's one linksman whose stunningly strong bond with his putter has caused him to reject all of his other clubs. Joseph Harris, 87, of Hollywood, Fla., loves his old Golf Pride Grand Slam putter so much that he won't use another club on the course!

He tees off with it, chips with it, pitches with it, and even extricates himself from sand traps with it. Oh, and there's one other thing: Harris has made 168 holes in one with it!

It sounds like fiction, but it isn't. Harris plays all his golf on the Pines Par-3 Golf Course in Hollywood, where every one of his aces has been witnessed.

Harris happened upon this unusual method by sheer whimsy. One day, he was standing in the middle of a fairway about 140 yards from the green when, for the heck of it, he whacked his approach shot with his putter. Harris hit the ball onto the putting surface. From then on, he was hooked. Harris dumped all his other clubs from his bag and he hasn't used anything but the blade since. "I like to be different," he said.

But Harris is the same as most duffers in one way. It usually takes him three or four putts to hole out. "That's the one thing I don't know how to do," lamented Harris. "I don't know how to putt."

Putt It in the Record Book

In 1990, an eight-handicapper named Denis C. Parker of Grand Prairie, Tex., had a round of 70 that included 14 one-putts. He two-putted twice and chipped in twice. That's strong, but it's not a record.

Fewest Putts in a Round

15—Richard Stanwood, 1976, Riverside Golf Club, Pocatello, Idaho.
15—Ed Drysdale, 1985, La Junta (Colo.) Golf Club.
17—Joan Joyce, 1982, Brookfield West Country Club, Roswell, Ga.

"I've gotten rid of the yips four times, but they hang in there. You know those two-foot downhill putts with a break? I'd rather see a rattlesnake."

—SAM SNEAD

> **"My putting touch usually deserts
> me under pressure. From
> five feet to the hole, you're
> in the throw up zone."**
>
> —DAVE HILL

No Putts, No Glory

Some players have such a deep-seated aversion to putting they will go to any lengths to keep off the green. One such player is Phillip A. Hays of Rochester, Minn. Hays hates putting so much that he developed a short game that is without peer—he holds the world record for chip-ins.

Hays's philosophy is simple: one way to keep from blowing a four-footer is to make the chip. He holed out an incredible 85 times in 1990, breaking his previous mark of 80 set in 1989. He chipped in 72 times at Soldiers Memorial Golf Course in his hometown and he drained 13 chips in and around Jacksonville, Fla.

Before Hays raised the chip-in to an art form, the one-year record of 64 had been held by J. Carl Plumlee of Little Rock, Ark.

This Game Can Drive You Buggy

Putting is tough enough, but Dr. H. J. Morland of Phoenix got one of the all-time bad breaks when his putt for birdie suddenly stopped dead on the lip. Upon examination, Dr. Morland found that an earthworm had come out of the cup and encircled the ball, keeping it out of the hole.

Another of God's little creatures was helpful to a linksman. In 1921 at the Scarborough South Cliff Course in Yorkshire, England, Paul McGregor needed only to sink a 20-foot putt to win the match. His heart sank as his putt hung on the lip and wouldn't fall. But just then, a grasshopper leaped onto the ball—and knocked it into the hole, giving McGregor the victory.

One Putt? It's a Locke

South African pro Bobby Locke might have been the greatest putter who ever lived, according to those who saw him. He beat Sam Snead 12 times out of 16 challenge matches played in South Africa. In 1947, the first of his two years in the United States, Locke won six of the 13 events he entered, placed second twice, and never finished lower than seventh.

The reason? "He was the most fabulous putter ever," marveled Gary Player. "There was no putt he couldn't make. No one has ever putted like that man."

Once asked which putt he preferred, a right-to-left breaker, a left-to-right breaker, or a dead-straight putt, Locke replied, "I've enjoyed them all."

In 1945, Locke went through an entire season of competitive golf without three-putting a single green. That was more than an estimated 1,800 consecutive holes!

Unfortunately, his putting streak happened before such records were kept. The official world record for the most consecutive holes without three-putting is 628, held by Rudolph Benavides, Jr., of Dallas, Tex. Benavides accomplished the feat from May 16 to July 26 in 1978.

Q. What is the longest putt in the history of the Masters?

A. 100 feet. Great Britain's Nick Faldo knocked in the astounding putt on the 3rd hole of the third round of the 1989 Masters.

goony golf

Some golfers love the sport so much that they play on and on in endurance matches that rival triathlons. Other linksmen are so obsessed they play golf without a course—by fashioning their own out of city streets. Then there are those who like to add bizarre twists to the sport such as playing in a suit of armor.

Long Day's Journey into Night

Ronald Kantner, a 30-year-old chiropractor from Wapakoneta, Ohio, holds the record for the most holes played on foot during a 24-hour period.

He wanted to find a fun way to raise money for the American Cancer Society, so, at a club pro's suggestion, Kantner decided to give marathon golf a shot. He figured it couldn't be any tougher than running, which he did regularly in minimarathons and 10K races around Wapakoneta.

In 1991, Kantner, a nine-handicapper, attempted to play more holes of golf in a 24-hour period than anyone had ever tried before on foot. It was not a perfect day for such a feat at the Wapakoneta Country Club, with a temperature of 93 degrees and the humidity at 90 percent.

Richard Kimbrough, who held the world mark of 364 holes in a day, offered Kantner advice and encouragement. "Richard told me that if I was going to break the record, I'd have to really make time during the daylight hours because the going at night would be really slow," Kantner recalled.

When he started, Kantner was virtually flying around the golf course, which was set up to play at 3,010 yards for nine holes, 6,020 yards for 18 holes. He averaged nine holes every 28 minutes—about three minutes a hole. At such a pace, he would have played a mind-boggling 480 holes in 24 hours. But keeping up that pace proved impossible.

Kantner slowed down considerably by nightfall, when he began using golf balls that glow in the dark but that fly only about 70 percent as far as regulation balls. By four a.m., Kantner began to feel the pain. His left knee collapsed, and he wasn't certain he could continue. "Things weren't too good at that point," he said. In addition to his ailing knee, huge blisters were forming on his feet. Four of his toenails were lost, and he had to stop for an hour. "By then, I had built in enough of a cushion so that I could take the break and still surpass the record," Kantner said.

> ### *"Pebble Beach is Alcatraz with grass."*
>
> —BOB HOPE, COMEDIAN

He caught his second wind and played on. When the clock struck noon, Kantner was in the books for the speed/endurance record for 24 hours of golf. Limping on bleeding feet but smiling broadly, Kantner played his 366th hole, two more than the previous mark. He had walked the equivalent of 78 miles, taken 2,134 strokes, shot an average 18-hole score of a little more than 105—and raised $5,400 for charity.

"I'm thinking about a few other records that might be reachable," Kantner said after the marathon. "But I'll have to heal up first. This was tougher than I thought it would be. But it was worth it."

Q. What is the world's longest golf course?

A. The par-77 International Golf Club at Bolton, Mass., is a whopping 8,325 yards long. That's 1,125 yards longer than the typical 7,200-yard par-72 championship layout.

Off Course

Bored golfers have dreamed up bizarre variations of the grand old game. Who needs a golf course?

• In 1929, brothers Clyde and Harold McWhirter played a long-distance match between Spartanburg and Union, S.C. The brothers covered the 37-mile distance in 13 hours. Clyde took 780 shots while Harold needed 825. The McWhirters lost 22 balls between them and used eight caddies.

• A pair of students at St. Andrews (Scotland) University teed off at Ceres, an inland Fifeshire village, and clubbed their golf balls until they arrived at the 18th hole on the Old Course at St. Andrews nine miles away.

The competitors, R.S. Little and K.G. Sherriff, had set some ground rules. Each used just one club and the ball could be teed up before each shot. The final rule: It would be no contest if one of them did not hole out in less than 300 strokes. After eight hours of competition, a pace better than a mile per hour, Little prevailed by two strokes, defeating Sherriff 236 to 238.

• Richard Sutton, a stockbroker, played out his fantasy of a cross-city golf excursion in London in 1939. Sutton made a wager that he could play from the Tower Bridge across town to White's Club on St. James Street in fewer than 200 strokes. Using a putter, Sutton crossed the Thames at the Southwark Bridge without hitting a ball into the water. Then he whacked away down the boulevards and through a park, and easily won the £100 bet by making it to White's Club in only 142 strokes.

• Four Aberdeen University students tried to golf their way up Scotland's 4,406-foot Mt. Ben Nevis in 1961. But they had to concede victory to the mountain. They quit after losing 63 balls and taking 659 strokes.

Have Your Club Call Our Club

The first known golf match by telephone was played in 1957 when the Cotswold Hills Golf Club of Cheltenham, England, challenged the Cheltenham Golf Club of Melbourne, Australia. The match was open to every member of both clubs and the aggregate score was phoned in to England. Cotswold beat Cheltenham, 564–570.

> ### *"Spyglass Hill is a 300-acre unplayable lie."*
>
> —JIM MURRAY, SPORTSWRITER

This Is Golf?

Golf sometimes isn't played quite the way it was intended. In fact, the golf course has been the scene of some weird versions of the sport.

- RAF pilot Capt. R. Pennington attempted a high-flying form of golf in 1933. He flew a thousand feet over Sonning Golf Course in England and dropped golf balls from his plane, hoping they would land on the greens. The balls were covered with cloth to minimize bouncing. Pennington needed 29 "shots," or balls, to hit all 18 greens.

- In a wacky handicap match at Wellington, England, a golfer played against a fisherman who used a rod equipped with a 25-ounce weight as his ball. Golfer Rupert May shot an 87 while angler J. J. Mackinlay netted a 102 in the 1913 contest. Although

Mackinlay consistently cast the weight over 100 yards straight and true on the fairway, he had trouble trying to hit the cup from short distances.

• F.M.A. Webster and his partner used javelins in a round against the great golfer Harry Vardon and his partner, who both played the normal way. Distances in the 1913 event were adjusted so that the javelin throwers had only to hit within a two-foot radius of the cup to hole out. The golfers easily prevailed, 5 and 4. Webster's longest drive, er, throw, was 160 feet.

> ## *"The Tournament Players Club [at Sawgrass] is 'Star Wars' golf. The place was designed by Darth Vader."*
>
> —BEN CRENSHAW

Fashion Mis-Statements

• Nigel Farrar played a round of golf in full battle gear. In 1914, just before World War I broke out, the English soldier made a bet that he could play the Royston Links in less than 100 strokes. Decked out in his full infantry gear, water bottle, field kit, and haversack, Farrar won the wager. He shot a 94.

• Englishman Harry Dearth played an entire round of golf clad in a complete suit of

armor! In 1912, he accepted a challenge match dressed in full
knight regalia and played at Bushey Hall in England where
he clanked to a 2 and 1 defeat.

• Capt. Gerald Moxom, an English officer, played
a round in formal attire. He wasn't going to let a small
matter like a wedding interfere with a club
championship. So on his wedding day in
1934, Moxom tied the knot, then hurried
from the chapel in Bournemouth, England,
to his golf club in West Hill, Surrey. Still
dressed in his tuxedo, Moxom shot a
round of 61 and won the competition.

Crossing the Finnish Line

Golfers can tee off in one country and hole out in another at the Green Zone Golf
Course near Haparanda, Sweden—the world's only two-nation golf course.

The 132-yard, par-3 6th hole straddles the Swedish-Finnish border so that the tee shot
is in Sweden and the hole is in Finland. It's the only course with a customs office and a

scorecard that includes customs regulations instead of ground rules. However, passports are not required for playing the course.

It can take over an hour just to make a four-foot putt on the 6th hole because the border that goes across the green divides not only the two countries but also two time zones.

Because the course is an hour from the Arctic Circle, the sun doesn't set during the summer, so golfers can play around the clock from June into August.

The Pacific Coast Open

The longest and perhaps strangest golf match in U.S. history took place in 1974, when a pair of California teenagers golfed their way from San Francisco to Los Angeles 387 miles away. Robert Aube, then 17, and Phil Marronne, then 18, set out along the shoulder of the famed Pacific Coast Highway.

They chopped away along the cliffs of Big Sur, into ice plants, thickets, and brush; through coastal towns of gawking residents; and across busy intersections. Sixteen days later, Aube and Marronne reached Los Angeles. The intrepid pair did not keep an accurate score. However, they did manage to figure out how many golf balls they had lost—more than 85 dozen!

New Meaning for Getting Up and Down

Jack Nicklaus holds the record for the most golf courses played in a single day by a pro golfer.

In January of 1991, the Golden Bear played 18 holes at 18 different golf courses in eight hours, 40 minutes to raise money for charity. Nicklaus crisscrossed Palm Beach County, Fla., in a helicopter, playing one hole per course. He shot 73, which was par for the 18.

The event raised $590,000—including a $500,000 donation from an anonymous Oklahoma physician.

Mind If We Play Through?

Walter Hagen, golf's dapper gentleman of the 1930s, and trick-shot artist Joe Kirkwood used to amuse themselves by driving golf balls through their hotel window into Central Park when they were staying in New York City. The pair would open a floor-length window, tee up balls, and whale away for hours.

When they grew bored with that, they came up with Boulevard Golf. They walked a few blocks from the hotel, dropped a ball, and began playing. The course was along the street, back to the hotel, through the lobby, up the elevator, down the hall, through their room, and into the commode.

"Hagen always made it back to the room first," Kirkwood once said. "But I always beat him. He could never master the in-the-bowl shot."

bag of tricks

Propelling a ball that is 1.68 inches in diameter and weighs 1.62 ounces into a hole that is 4.25 inches across from a distance of some 200 yards away can be very difficult under the best conditions.

But imagine hitting a ball blindfolded, or on one leg, or hitting three golf balls at once—and sending them in different directions to the spots where you wanted them to land. Those are the kinds of phenomenal shots made by a very small number of experts—the trick-shot artists.

Tricksters' Trickiest Trick Shots

• Paul Hahn, one of the greatest trick-shot artists of all time, had a repertoire of 30 trick shots. His most confounding trick involved hitting two balls simultaneously, one with his right hand and the other with his left, making one ball hook and the other ball slice.

• Following in his father's footsteps, Paul Hahn, Jr., has wowed fans by hitting three golf balls with one swing. One ball flies straight ahead, one scoots backward, and the third pops up in the air—and lands right in the palm of Hahn's hand.

• Joe Kirkwood, the legendary Aussie trickster of the 1930s, used to tee a golf ball on the flat side of a Hershey's Kiss held between the teeth of an attractive female assistant.

With a flourish, Kirkwood would safely whack his drive and then kiss his assistant, much to the delight of the audience.

• E. A. Forrest blindfolded himself after a ball was teed up on the chin of his assistant. Forrest never failed to hit a clean shot. And he kept the same assistant for years—uninjured.

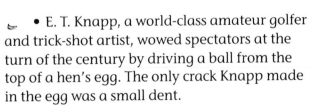

• E. T. Knapp, a world-class amateur golfer and trick-shot artist, wowed spectators at the turn of the century by driving a ball from the top of a hen's egg. The only crack Knapp made in the egg was a small dent.

Too Much Iron in His Blood

As a boy growing up in Pedrena, Spain, Seve Ballesteros practiced with a three-iron, the only club available to him. Using that club in a variety of ways enabled Ballesteros to develop one of the greatest golfing imaginations in the world today.

"You learn to do everything with that club," Ballesteros said. "It makes you think things up that you never would if you had all the clubs."

And he can prove it. Even now, when he's in the mood during rain delays, Ballesteros will demonstrate his prowess with the club. Once, during a PGA Tour stop in Fort Lauderdale, Ballesteros dropped several balls in a greenside bunker and took out his three-iron. He told fellow pros Ben Crenshaw and Leonard Thompson that he could get the ball as close to the pin with that club as they could with their sand wedges. He outshot them three out of four tries.

"It's one of the most amazing things I've ever seen anyone do with a golf club," Crenshaw said.

> *"I would rather play Hamlet with no rehearsal than play golf on television."*
>
> —JACK LEMMON, ACTOR

A Standing Record

In 1980, not a particularly exciting year in Charlotte, N.C., Lang Martin balanced seven golf balls vertically without aid of adhesive.

This broke the previous mark of six, also set by Martin, in 1967.

Q. What was the smallest club ever used?

A. Trick-shot artist Joe Kirkwood swung the world's tiniest golf club—a wedge that was only 18 inches long! The trickster also wielded the longest club—a 10-foot driver.

Amazing But True Lies

• In a tourney, Aubrey Boomer was playing the 8th hole at St. Anne's Golf Course in Scotland in 1923 when he lost sight of the ball after launching an approach shot straight up in the air. A search proved unsuccessful and officials were prepared to hand Boomer a penalty for losing his ball. But then the startled golfer felt a solid object in the right-hand pocket of his jacket. He reached in—and produced the missing ball!

• Amateur Jim Smith hit a wayward shot that landed in another golfer's pocket! In 1991, Jim Smith was playing at the Fort Dodge (Iowa) Country Club when his nine-iron shot on the 6th hole landed in the pocket of startled golfer Jim Van Gundy, who was waiting to tee off on the 7th hole. "I felt a little nick on my left thigh," Van Gundy recalled. "I tried to find the ball for the guy but couldn't. Then I put my hand in the pocket of my shorts and found the ball. I couldn't believe it."

• Elvin Wilson pulled the old hidden ball trick during a 1986 golf match at Hawaii's Makena Golf Course. Playing a tough shot atop lava rocks, Wilson swung his club. He and his playing partners watched the ball ricochet off a rock and then seemingly disappear. To everyone's amazement, Wilson reached under his armpit and produced the ball!

• A case of flag-waving resulted in a birdie for pro Bobby Locke at the Irish Open in 1936. His tee shot at the 100-yard 12th hole appeared to be lost, until someone shook the flagstick. Locke's ball had become entangled in the flag! It fell to the green a few inches from the hole and Locke tapped it in for the birdie.

• Penance was two strokes for Bob Roos of San Francisco, who was playing golf one Sunday morning in 1958 when his ball went to church. Roos overclubbed his approach shot, causing the ball to spin off a hard spot near the green and bounce over a fence. The ball then zipped across the street—and through the open door of a church!

• During a Royal and Ancient tournament at St. Andrews, Scotland, in 1907, a member of the R & A drove a ball that struck the sharp point of a hat pin in the hat of a woman who was crossing the course. The ball was so firmly impaled on the pin that it stayed anchored to the woman's hat! The woman was unhurt.

Follow the Bouncing Ball

Have you ever tried bouncing a golf ball on the face of a sand wedge to see how many times you can do it without messing up? It's not easy.

In 1990, Rob MacGregor, head professional at the Blenheim Community Golf Club in Ontario, bounced a ball on the face of his left-handed wedge 3,699 times.

He blew away the record set back in 1985, when Mark Mooney of Hummlestown, Pa., wore out the face of his pitching wedge by bouncing a ball on it 1,764 times.

> *"The difference between golf and government is that in golf you can't improve your lie."*
>
> —GEORGE DEUKMEJIAN,
> FORMER GOVERNOR OF CALIFORNIA

the over-the-hill gang

Even when you're on the back side of 35, you can still shoot 35 on the back side. That's part of the timeless appeal of golf. It's the sport in which you're never too old to succeed, never too crusty to conjure up the skills that could produce a personal best.

Ben Hogan, after all, won the first of his four U.S. Opens when he was 36 years old. At age 46, Jack Nicklaus shot 30 on the back nine at Augusta National to complete a blazing 65 that won him his sixth Masters. Raymond Floyd was 44 when he won his first U.S. Open title, becoming the oldest man ever to win that tournament until Hale Irwin won his third Open title at the age of 45. Not even the U.S. Amateur is immune. The tourney, usually the province of fuzzy-cheeked college kids on their way to the PGA Tour, was won in 1991 by 41-year-old Mitch Voges.

The Methuselah of the Links

Arthur Thompson was the oldest golfer who ever lived. He was still playing golf competitively on his 103rd birthday in 1973. On that day, he become the oldest man in history to equal his age on the golf course, shooting 103 at Uplands Golf Course in Ontario, Canada, near his home.

Of course, being the oldest linksman was old hat for Thompson. For nearly a decade, he remained the oldest man to have bettered his age, shooting in the 90s on several occasions.

Thompson scored in the 70s more than 100 times while he was in his 80s. At the age of 89, he shot a round of 82. When he was well into his 90s, Thompson was hitting drives that traveled more than 200 yards. All of his best scores were shot at Uplands, a challenging course measuring more than 6,215 yards.

Shortly before his death in 1975 at the age of 105, he still enjoyed playing nine holes.

Q. Who is the youngest golfer to win the Masters?
A. Seve Ballesteros. He won the 1980 Masters by four strokes—at the tender age of 23 years, 4 days.

Under Age Seniors

The all-time record for shooting the most strokes under one's age is held by George M. Smith of Fort Myers, Fla. At the age of 90, he shot an astonishing 75—15 strokes under his age—at the 6,009-yard Cypress Lake Golf Club in Fort Myers, Fla., in 1988. No one has come close to the record since.

This Barber Shaves Strokes

Jerry Barber, 74, is one of the most amazing golfers alive. Even though he's the oldest active competitor on the Senior PGA Tour, he can still compete with the Tour's 50- and 60-year-old whippersnappers.

In 1990, during Senior Tour events, Barber bettered his age an astounding 25 times, and equalled it another 13 times. Although he already was 65 when the Senior Tour first came into existence in 1981, he had earned nearly $500,000 by the end of his 10th season.

Barber's resilience is really remarkable. He was on the road for 33 weeks in both the 1990 and 1991 seasons.

"What am I supposed to do, retire?" he asked. "I already play golf and fish almost every day. And I'm getting paid for the golf. Got any better ideas?"

The Magic Number is 59

The number 59 is a sacred one in golfing circles. It is the lowest score ever shot under tournament conditions, and it has been matched only twice—by Al Geiberger in the 1977 Danny Thomas Memphis Classic and by Chip Beck in the 1991 Las Vegas Invitational.

Incredibly, two other golfers shot that stunning score of 59—at the age of 59! They are Bob Hamilton and Malcom Miller, the youngest golfers ever to shoot their age.

Hamilton, a professional, had his sizzling round of 13 under par in 1975 at the 6,233-yard Hamilton Golf Club in Evansville, Ind. Miller, an amateur, shot his 59 at the 6,118-yard Minocqua (Wis.) Country Club in 1977. In the years since, no other golfer (other than Beck) has come within three shots of their feat.

Senior golfer Spec Goldman, on how he reads greens:

***"If I'm breathing heavy while walking on a green,
I'm going uphill.
If I trip, I'm going downhill."***

The (Near) Dead Golfers Society

In 1991, the world's oldest living foursome of avid golfers totaled 361 years of age. The foursome included Maurice Pease, 98, Joe Hooker, 94, Richardson Bronson, 85, and Stanley Hart, Sr., 84. The golfing geezers have played a round of golf together every week since 1981 at the Country Club of New Bedford (Mass.).

Better with Age

Although he had long since quit competing in 1977, Ben Hogan remained a super golfer. He managed to shoot his age for the first time at the age of 64. And he did it on one of the longest and toughest golf courses in Texas, the 6,975-yard Shady Oaks Country Club in Fort Worth. Amazingly, Hogan's longtime rival, Sam Snead, bettered his age for the first time that same year. Snead, then 64, fired a 63 at the Costa del Sol Golf Course in Miami.

"The older I get, the easier it is," said Snead, now 78 and still playing. "I think I'll be able to shoot in the 70s until the day they lay me out."

Time Is on Their Side

Players often dominate their club championships, but few can keep their skills sharpened for 40 or more years and win club titles in each decade of their adulthood. Here are the national record holders for club championships, all of whom have won titles in each of *six* decades:

- William R. Kramer, St. Clair Country Club, Pittsburgh.
- Harold Foreman, Lake Shore Country Club, Glencoe, Ill.
- Clarence C. Randall, Logan (Utah) Country Club.
- Frances Cary Whyte, Sequoyah Country Club, Oakland, Calif.
- Lib Bryan, New Bern (N.C.) Golf & Country Club.

> *"As a golfer ages, the fairways get longer and the holes get smaller."*
>
> —BOBBY LOCKE

The Golden Bear's Golden Age

Now in his 50s, Jack Nicklaus holds virtually every championship record worth having in golf—including a very significant United States Golf Association mark.

With his victory in the 1991 U.S. Senior Open, Nicklaus is the first golfer to have won at least one USGA event in each of five decades. His streak began in 1959 when he won the U.S. Amateur (which he also won in 1961). He finished first in the U.S. Open in 1962, 1967, 1972, and 1980.

The closest anyone else has come to winning a major USGA competition in five separate decades is Anne Sander, who has won USGA events throughout four decades. She finished first in the Women's Amateur in 1958, 1961, and 1963, and she won the Senior Women's Amateur in 1987, 1988, and 1990.

> **"Like a lot of fellows on the Senior Tour, I have a furniture problem. My chest has fallen into my drawers."**
>
> —BILLY CASPER

Turning Back the Callender

F. L. Callender, formerly of St. Andrews, Scotland, was the oldest golfer ever to reach the finals of an important match play tournament. At the age of 78, in 1932, Callender shocked the local citizenry by winning eight consecutive matches in his quest for the Jubilee Vase. The trophy was awarded to the winner of the grueling match play competition at the Old Course at St. Andrews.

Although Callender was defeated in the finals, 4 and 2, his was the most impressive performance by a septuagenarian in top-level competition until nearly 60 years later when 75-year-old Jerry Barber nearly won a Senior PGA Tour event.

when bad things happen to good golfers

When it comes to golfing disasters, no one explained it better than the great Bobby Jones, *a player who, ironically, experienced very few. He once said:*

"On the golf course, a man can be the dogged victim of inexorable fate, be struck down by an appalling stroke of tragedy, become the hero of an unbelievable melodrama, or the clown in a side-splitting comedy—any of these within a few hours, and all without having to bury a corpse or repair a tangled personality."

Jones was speaking for weekend duffers and touring pros alike.

Shark Attacked

Good luck for others often means bad luck for Greg Norman.

In 1986, Bob Tway holed out from a bunker 22 feet away on the final hole of the PGA Championship to deny the Shark. In the 1987 Masters, a miracle 40-yard pitch by Larry Mize in sudden death beat Norman. A textbook five-iron shot from the rough for birdie by Mark Calcavecchia vanquished Norman in a playoff at the 1989 British Open. Then, in 1990, there was the miracle 172-yard seven-iron on the 72nd hole from the fairway by Robert Gamez at Bay Hill Country Club in Orlando. It was for an eagle and Norman lost by a shot. A few weeks later, David Frost holed a bunker shot at the final hole at New Orleans to beat Norman by one shot. All of Greg's bad karma started at an obscure tournament in 1982. He was cruising along near the lead in the Martini International at Lindrick Golf Club in England when he was victimized by a thoughtless photographer.

Norman was on a roll, coming off three straight birdies as he teed up at the 17th hole. At the top of Norman's swing, a motor drive in a camera began whirring and distracted the golfer. Unable to stop his swing, the Shark sent his drive screaming into the woods to the left of the fairway. The lie was virtually unplayable, but Norman believed he could hit most any shot—including this one.

He thrashed at the ball, which then hit a branch and bounced into a lie that was impossible, even for him. He took a drop. That lie wasn't much better. A mighty swing moved the ball just a few feet into another unplayable lie. Norman dropped again. His next effort screamed deep into a thicket, forcing him to take another penalty stroke. He tried to hit the ball

out of the woods. Unfortunately, just as it was about to clear the trees, the ball struck the last remaining limb and ricocheted straight down into the thicket.

Finally, Norman dropped another ball and pitched out sideways onto the fairway. His approach missed the green. He chipped on and took two putts for his highest score ever as a pro on one hole—14.

> *"It took me 17 years to get 3,000 hits in baseball. I did it in one afternoon on the golf course."*
>
> —BASEBALL HALL OF FAME SLUGGER HANK AARON

A Real Lemmon

He has won Oscars, dined with royalty, schmoozed with presidents, and partied with the most famous people in Hollywood. But Jack Lemmon has never played golf on Sunday at Pebble Beach in the final round of the AT&T Pebble Beach National Pro-Am (which for years was known as The Crosby).

In 21 years of trying, Lemmon has failed to make the cut for the final 18. This failure gnaws on him so much that he insists he would trade some of his fame and fortune for the chance to play in the final round.

Alas, Lemmon's game simply will not permit it. He is the essence of the frustrated high-handicapper. He has read every book and bought every club, all to no avail. But at least, in his embarrassments, he has garnered a few laughs.

"Two incidents stand out," Lemmon recalled. "First was the time I was playing at Cypress Point with Peter Jacobsen and Clint Eastwood. I hit my ball on the 16th to the edge of the cliff. Eastwood looks down at the ball hanging in the ice plant and says, 'Hit the son of a bitch.' Well, if I try to hit it, I fall down the cliff and die. So Eastwood grabs the back of my pants and Peter grabs the back of Eastwood's and we form this human chain and I take a swing and the ball comes out just short of the green. It's a wonderful shot. I go up there ready to chip it on. And I'm waggling the club and drinking it all in. And then I shank the next shot off the cliff and into the ocean."

Another time, Lemmon was struggling well over par and definitely about to miss another cut when the red light on the TV camera came on. A true actor, Lemmon was determined at least to look like a golfer even though he was on the green putting for a sextuple bogey.

"I'm lying about 10 and I've got a 35-footer," he recalled. "I'm lining this thing up, trying to make a decent show. I whisper over my shoulder to the caddie, 'Which way does this break?' And he says, 'Who cares?' Greatest single line I've ever heard from a caddie."

Legendary golf writer Bernard Darwin,
swearing loudly at God after being unable
to extricate himself from a bunker:

**_"And don't send your Son down.
This is a man's job."_**

Jinx on the Links

Gene Sarazen hit a once-in-a-lifetime drive that should have landed within six feet of the cup at the 1936 Western Open. But Sarazen's great shot bounced a few feet from the pin and struck the ball of his playing partner, Jimmy Demaret. Sarazen's ball then skipped into a nearby lake. Demaret birdied the par-3 hole, while the disgusted Sarazen had to settle for a six. That put him out of contention.

Mother Nature played a mean trick on pro Chuck Rotar at the 1961 Orange County (Cal.) Open. He had just made a nice approach shot onto the 18th green when the area was hit with a mild earthquake. Unfortunately, the tremor shook his ball downhill and into a pond. Rotar had to drop a new ball and take a penalty stroke. He finished with a double bogey on the hole.

Know (It) Thyself

The top rules official in golf incurred a penalty—and didn't even realize it when he committed the violation.

David Eger, who had replaced the late P. J. Boatright as the senior director of rules and competition for the USGA, was playing a qualifying round for the U.S. Mid-Amateur Championship in 1991 when his fellow competitor hit a ball deep into the woods. The golfer played a provisional ball onto the green, and then he and Eger began the search for the first ball.

After they tromped around for close to the allowed five minutes, Eger turned to his playing partner and said, "If I were you, I'd play the provisional."

Oops. A USGA official, who was accompanying the golfers, slapped the embarrassed Eger with a two-stroke penalty for violating Rule 8–1, which states, "A player shall not give advice to anyone in the competition."

Eger learned there's no surer or more painful way to remember a rule than to be penalized for breaking it.

A Staggering Start

Colorful Irish pro Christy O'Connor, Jr., found himself in a predicament at the 1963 World Cup at St. Nom la Breteche near Paris. It was nearly tee time and he could barely see—because, as he later admitted, he was terribly hung over from partying the night before.

He was rousted in the locker room by Mark Wilson, the golf correspondent for London's *Daily Express*. Wilson informed the bleary-eyed O'Connor that his tee time was imminent and he might want to put his shoes on and make his way to the first tee. O'Connor reluctantly staggered to his feet and told Wilson to get a large mug of black coffee. "Pace off 65 yards from the 200-yard post on the first hole and wait for me there in the woods," said the golfer.

Wilson got the coffee and headed for the woods while O'Connor stumbled off to the tee. When his turn came to hit, Christy launched a 265-yard drive into the woods. Wilson watched the ball rattle around in the trees and drop a few feet from where he stood. Moments later, O'Connor arrived. The Irishman chugged the coffee, thanked his friend, and pressed on. Christy managed to shoot three under par that day, a remark-able score—given the circumstances.

Brooks, Trees, and Lakes

Mark Brooks was competing in the 1991 Las Vegas Invitational when he learned exactly what Bob Jones meant about "dogged victims of inexorable fate."

Brooks was cruising along at 12 under par after two rounds, and he knew that a good weekend in the 90-hole tournament would mean a big payday. He started on the 10th hole, and when he arrived at the 17th he was even for the day. Then he walked through the door of golf's twilight zone.

Brooks hit his tee shot into a tree—but the ball never came down. No problem. Since Brooks needed to identify his ball before he could declare it unplayable and drop another, a nearby cherry picker was summoned to the scene. The golfer climbed into the basket and was raised into the tree, where he pulled eight balls from the branches. Unfortunately, none of the balls were his.

So Brooks had to return to the tee and wound up making a double bogey seven on the relatively easy par-5 hole. But that wasn't the end of his troubles. The next day, he was on the green at the par-3 9th hole with a good chance for a birdie. Brooks marked his ball and tossed it to his caddie to clean. Taken by surprise, the caddie missed the throw and the ball whizzed past his hand and splashed into the lake.

Determined not to be penalized again, Brooks shed his shoes, his socks, and his shirt and went into the hazard looking for his golf ball. He came up with 18 balls. But none of them were his.

Dripping wet and steaming mad, Brooks putted out with another ball and added two penalty shots for finishing with a ball other than the one he had started with.

It was no surprise that Brooks finished the tournament dead last. Said the dejected golfer, "When you're climbing trees and splashing around in the water, you know things are not going your way."

> *"If I swung a gavel the way I swung that golf club, the nation would be in a helluva mess."*
>
> —TIP O'NEILL,
> FORMER SPEAKER OF THE HOUSE

holing out

The great sportswriter Grantland Rice once said, *"Golf is 20 percent mechanics and techniques. The other 80 percent is philosophy, humor, tragedy, romance, melodrama, companionship, camaraderie, cussedness, and conversation."* Here are some amazing golfing moments to talk about:

Rarest of Rara Avis

There is no shot more difficult in golf than the double eagle, the albatross—a two on a par-5 hole or an ace on a par-4. The odds of making such a shot are 1 in 5.85 million. But what are the odds of scoring two albatrosses on the same hole in the same day? Virtually incalculable, although Xiaobao Wang, a statistics consultant at the University of California-Berkeley, figures them at 1 in 34,200,000,000,000 (34.2 trillion).

Against those odds, amateur John Cook, 27, did just that. In 1990 at the Ocean Course on Hilton Head Island, he bagged a pair of albatrosses on the 475-yard, par-5 14th hole, a difficult dogleg. In the morning, he used a three-wood and an eight-iron to make a two. In the afternoon, he hit a three-wood and a wedge!

Thus Cook became only the second man in recorded history to score two double eagles on the same hole in the same day. Previously, only Oscar McCash, Jr., in 1983 at the

471-yard, par-5 8th hole at Decatur (Tex.) Country Club, had accomplished the stunning feat.

The longest double eagle ever recorded came on the 609-yard par-5 15th hole at Makaha Inn West Course in Hawaii in 1972, where amateur John Eakin of California twice used a driver to hole out in two.

Addicted to Golf

Anyone who has played a round of golf can testify to the powerfully addictive traits of the sport. But no one has been smitten by the narcotic effect more than Merle Ball, 72, of Sebring, Fla. She plays during just about every waking moment. And that's no exaggeration.

In the first seven months of 1991, Ball had played 10,800 holes of golf—about 600 rounds—shattering the unofficial amateur record of 542 rounds in a single year. During that span, she averaged almost 54 holes per day, seven days a week!

Ball once played a marathon 220 holes in 13 hours—half left-handed and half right-handed. She performed her astonishing feat at the Sun 'N Lake Golf and Country Club at Sebring, Fla., in 1990. A natural righty, Ball averaged scores of 46 per nine holes right-handed and 48 left-handed.

> *"Golf is . . . the most useless outdoor game ever devised to waste the time and try the spirit of man."*
>
> —WESTBROOK PEGLER, SPORTSWRITER

Super Ball

The record for frugality in golf goes to Bruce Reagan of Mobile, Ala., who somehow managed to play 14 rounds of golf—284 consecutive holes—using the same golf ball.

Reagan played the Pinnacle Gold ball throughout the rounds at Azalea City Golf Course in Mobile, Ala., and Cairo (Ga.) Country Club. His streak ended when the ball developed a crack in it.

Incredibly, the ball wasn't even new when Reagan started his string. He had found the ball in a water hazard!

About Face

The difference between the scores on the front and back nine in an 18-hole round usually is no more than a few strokes, but there are exceptions.

The most unbelievable recovery in history occurred in 1982, when amateur Matt Pace of Houston gave new meaning to the term "turning it around."

Playing a tournament at the 6,583-yard El Dorado Country Club in Humble, Tex., Pace shot an awful 64 on the front nine. His best hole was a bogey. Rather than withdraw, Pace played on—but he looked like an entirely different golfer. On the back nine, he shot a one-under-par 35 that included one bogey, six pars, and two birdies. Pace finished the day with 64–35—99. That astounding turnaround of 29 strokes is a world record. The previous record was 27, set in 1935 by Lawrence G. Knowles, who shot 63–36—99 at the Agawam Hunt Country Club in East Providence, R.I.

The flip side to those achievements is the turnaround orchestrated by Earl W. Gray in 1958 at Scioto Country Club, in Columbus, Ohio. Gray, of Overland Park, Kan., had just bogeyed the 9th for an outward score of 34, two under par. He was three under and on his way to a career round by the time he reached the 12th hole. But then disaster struck.

Gray was about 90 yards from the green when he hit the first shank of his life. He was so upset that he shanked his next three shots and wound up carding a 10 on the hole.

Gray then shanked every short-iron shot coming in and posted an embarrassing 64 for the back nine—a mortifying 30-shot turnaround for the worse.

Said Gray, "I love tennis—maybe I'll stick to that."

Q. How much money did the all-time great Bobby Jones win?

A. Nothing. Despite being a world-class golfer and a four-time winner of the U.S. Open, Jones never won any money in golf. He remained an amateur throughout his remarkable career and never accepted money for winning a tournament.

> ### *"Golf is a game in which you yell 'Fore,' shoot six, and write down five."*
>
> —PAUL HARVEY, NEWS COMMENTATOR

A Chip Off the Old Block

At the age of nine, Ben Crenshaw already was demonstrating superior athletic abilities, mainly as a baseball player. Ben's dad, an avid golfer, decided his son should try the game and took him over to Austin (Tex.) Country Club, where Harvey Penick, the legendary teacher, was the pro.

Penick took young Ben out to the fairway about 100 yards from the hole, gave him a club, and told the boy to hit the ball. Ben knocked the ball onto the green. "That's fine, Ben," Penick said. "Now let's go up and see you knock it in the hole."

Ben looked quizzically at his instructor and said, "Golly, Mr. Penick, why didn't you tell me that in the first place?" Ben then dropped another ball—and knocked it right into the cup!

Q. What is the lowest score for four consecutive rounds in tournament golf history?
A. A blistering 27-under-par 257, shot by Mike Souchak at Brackenridge Park Golf Club in San Antonio, Tex., in 1955. Souchak fired rounds of 60–68–64–65.

Not So Sudden Death

In pro golf, the longest "sudden death" playoffs in history lasted 13 extra holes. It has happened twice—both at the World Match Play Championships. In the 1960 playoff, W. S. Collins needed the extra holes to defeat W. J. Branch. The following year, Peter Alliss and Harold Henning played 13 additional holes before Henning won.

But they don't hold the record for tournament play. That mark was set by amateurs.

An exhausting 23-hole marathon playoff in the 1991 Tennessee Golf Association State Four-Ball Championship at Holston Hills Country Club in Knoxville was needed to determine a winner.

In the playoff, Ted Arsenault and Dale Rutherford defeated Chip Carlen and Martin Foutch after 41 grueling holes of play (including the regular 18-hole match). Said Arsenault, "There was a point where we didn't care. It got old after playing that many holes."

The four-ball marathon broke the previous record of 14 holes set in 1983 when a pair of twosomes battled 14 extra holes. The prize received by Jerry Spaeth and Chris Spaeth for winning their flight at the Glen Oak Country Club championship in Glen Ellyn, Ill., was a pair of golf shoes.

> *"Golf does strange things to people. It makes liars out of honest men, cheats out of altruists, cowards out of brave men, and fools out of everybody."*
>
> —MILTON GROSS, AUTHOR

Q. Who is the slowest player on the PGA Tour?

A. Bernhard "Nobody Takes" Langer. While the typical tour player takes an average of 35 seconds per shot, Langer averages 59 seconds. And on the greens, Langer turns into a statue. It takes him an average of 85.2 seconds to stroke a putt.

Armed to Win

Joshua Lee Patton, a former bar bouncer, has one of the most unorthodox golf swings in the world. An old knife wound to the stomach prevents Patton from using his left arm in a golf swing. So he has developed a windmill method with his right arm that he believes is the most effective one-armed technique in the United States.

Holding the club with only his right hand, Patton whips the club in a full circle and routinely wallops drives of more than 260 yards. One of his ultralong, one-armed hits went 335 yards! He claims to hit 4,000 practice balls a day, and currently plays with a handicap of 10. In 1989—only 15 months after taking up the game—Patton finished fourth in the World One-Armed Golf Championships in West Kilbride, Scotland.

After beating all the other American entrants, Patton boasted, "I'm the best one-armed golfer in America. And anyone who wants to test me can put up $5,000 and we'll play." The winnings, Patton insisted, would go to charity.

Q. Has anyone ever recorded consecutive double eagles?

A. Only one known golfer in history has scored back-to-back albatrosses. Amateur Norman L. Manley did it in 1964 when he nailed two consecutive holes-in-one on two par-4 holes—the 330-yard 7th hole and the 290-yard 8th hole at Del Valley Country Club in Saugus, Cal.

Toughing It Out

Golfers usually don't play with pain. The slightest injury can alter a swing almost imperceptibly with disastrous results. Still, when a man has to make a living, sometimes he does what he has to do—regardless of the potentially embarrassing consequences.

Pity poor Chick Evans. He injured his right forearm before the final round of the $1.5 million 1991 Vantage Championship at Tanglewood Park, Clemmons, N.C., the richest event on the Senior PGA Tour. Most players would have withdrawn with such an injury. But Evans, who wasn't one of the more successful players on the Tour, refused to quit. "Frankly," he explained, "I needed the money."

Last place in the Vantage paid $1,000. But in order to receive any winnings on the Senior PGA Tour, players must complete all of the holes in any given event. Since Evans had made just $26,000 up to that point, he played on for the thousand bucks.

The only way Evans could play was to hit every shot with a seven-iron. It was a toss-up as to what was more painful to watch—Evans chopping around the difficult Tanglewood course with a seven-iron or the number of shots that he ultimately put on the scoreboard at the end of the day.

The final tally was 126 strokes—a record high 18-hole score for the Senior Tour.

"I'm embarrassed," Evans said. "But you have to play to get paid. A thousand dollars is a thousand dollars. It's worth it."